Big Babies

Jacqueline McQuade

DAVID BENNETT BOOKS

Bear
Cub

A baby bear is called a cub.
This brave bear cub is climbing a tree
for the very first time.

Elephant
Calf

A baby elephant is called a calf.
This elephant calf is finding out how much fun
it is to have a trunk.

Lion Cubs

A baby lion is called a cub.
These lion cubs love to play rough-and-tumble
together in the warm sunshine.

Baby Gorilla

A baby gorilla does not have a special name.
*This baby gorilla feels warm and safe curled up
in his mummy's arms.*

Hippo
Calf

A baby hippo is called a calf.
This happy little hippo calf has swimming lessons
with her mummy every day.

Zebra
Foal

A baby zebra is called a foal.
This stripy zebra foal is taking her first steps
through the long grass.

Giraffe Calf

A baby giraffe is called a calf.
*This graceful giraffe calf is learning to look after herself,
but just now she still needs her mummy's help.*

Panda
Cubs

A baby panda is called a cub.
*These playful panda cubs are enjoying some
tasty bamboo shoots for their lunch.*